"The greatest love you can show is to give your life for your friends." (John 15:13 GWT)

The fifth commandment says, "Honor thy father and mother that thy days may be long upon the land which the Lord thy God giveth thee." (Exodus 20:12 KJV)

Having patience really is a virtue.

I witnessed Lennie's Love first hand and I loved and honored Lennie the best way that I knew how.

One of her favorite words was stickability; a person's ability to persevere with something; staying power.

Lennie's Love
Loving Lennie
A BEAUTIFUL LIFE

GREGORY W. MOAK

ISBN-13: 978-1508865698

Dedication

In loving memory of my mother, the one who gave me life without birth and loved me unconditionally. I have inherited her joy for loving and serving others and for that I will be eternally grateful.

Acknowledgments

With great love for Bolivar and Dorothy Sheridan, Lawrence and Emma Baylot, Bennie McBride, Buddy Casey, Byron Schilling, David and Janet Womack, John and Cheryl Douglas, Woodrow and Dolly Hobgood, Viola Wehmeyer, Charlie Case, and Perry and Tonya Hancock who, along with countless others, have provided encouragement and pointed me to the cross.

A Word From The Author

The greatest love a person can have for others is to give his life for them. (John 15:13 GWT) And, that is exactly what my mother, Lennie Marie Wascom Moak did for me. She gave her life. And, she did so in many ways.

Her love for me began with my adoption and continued by the way she lovingly cared and provided, by her guidance and support, and even loving me until her very last breath.

Our love for each other seemed to be at its pinnacle in those last six years together.

There will be many names and memories shared, but this is a story about a woman, a wife, a mother who simply loved not only her family, but her church family and friends, and those with whom she came in contact on a daily basis.

This is also a story about my love for her. When I returned home to care for her, I had no idea what being a caregiver would entail. I loved her, and felt in my heart it was the right thing to do.

I miss her dearly. To see her reaching out to me for one more hug. She frequently reached out to hug for no reason other than to be hugged and loved. But, mostly she reached out when I would return home. It didn't matter where I had been, or how long I had been gone. In her eyes, I had been gone way too long.

Oh, to be able to tell her one more time that I love her. All the things we wish we could do or say after they are gone.

To do so would be so wonderful. But, I am comforted in knowing that she is resting in the arms of Jesus. And, one day, only God knows that day, I shall see her again. I shall hug and kiss her again. I shall see her beautiful smile again. But, most importantly, she and I will be eternally together with Jesus.

Table of Contents

1 *The Early Years*

Mother's early childhood years were spent growing up in Bonner Creek, a small community in Louisiana located between Franklinton and Folsom. She was the youngest of Delos and Ouida Wascom's five children - Exie, Iris, T.J., Clyde, and Lennie.

Mother loved to tell people "no telling how many kids mom and dad might have had, we were coming along every two years like clockwork." It was also an easy way to figure out each other's ages.

I never met either of these grand-parents. Delos died of appendicitis when Mother was only seven months old, and Ouida died three years before I was born.

Aunt Exie and her husband Elvie never had children. They lived on a dairy farm out in the middle of nowhere. Their front yard was spacious enough to throw a football or a baseball just as far as one could possibly throw a ball.

The dairy fields went on forever. With all this space to run about, seemingly the first place I wanted to run to when I jumped out of the car was the hayloft. There was just something magical about climbing the ladder up into the loft full of stacked bales of hay. So many places to hide; to daydream for hours on end.

Aunt Exie's was a place to truly feel carefree. A place of freedom to run and play till you had no more energy. To play until you were called inside for lunch or dinner. And, if we were lucky enough to stay overnight, we would get up and do it all over again the next day. Though I loved playing there, for whatever reason, I can never remember volunteering to milk the cows.

Aunt Iris and her husband Buster Burkhalter had three children, Buster Roy, Ann and Rusty. They lived about three miles outside of Franklinton, just off the main highway to Amite. Lots of open space to play here as well, and they too had a hayloft in which to hang out for hours on end.

I remember during the 60's, Uncle Buster and Aunt Iris owned a cafe in Franklinton, the Minute Grill Café, located just off the main highway running through town. I loved going there. We had all the cheeseburgers and fries one could eat, plus Aunt Iris would give us change from the cash register to play the jukebox. Those were the days.

Uncle T.J. and his wife Jeanette had three children, Sue, Jesse Wayne and Kim. They lived in the Bonner Creek community close to the old home place.

Uncle T.J. was a very likeable person. He loved his family. He was hardworking and a military veteran who served in WWII.

Jeanette was happy-go-lucky. Always ready with a funny joke. She always made me laugh. She passed away in July of 1983, and later on, T.J. married Louise Jones.

Louise was a very outgoing person. She was devoted to family. Loved Jesus and loved sharing His love with children.

It was good for Louise and T.J. to share life together until his death in October 1993. Louise later passed away in October 2009, after a short battle with cancer.

Uncle Clyde was married to Geraldine McDaniel. They lived on Main Street in Franklinton. Never having had any children, they were the proud parents, so to speak, of over 1,000 different varieties of daylilies. It was their pride and joy along with their well-manicured yard, frequently winning "yard of the month" honors. In the prime of their lives, they loved being outdoors, working in their yard.

During my time home with Mother, we would visit with Uncle Clyde and Aunt Gerry at least once, sometimes twice, a week. Of the five siblings, she and Clyde were the only two remaining, and I sensed how important it was for both of them to be together as much as possible.

How ironic that Uncle Clyde was a victim of Alzheimer's and Mother fell prey to dementia.

Clyde endured until he fell and broke his hip. He went into surgery the night of his fall and never woke up. Aunt Gerry and many family and friends, including Mother and I, were by his side for nine days until his final breath on the 25th January, 2012.

2   *Lennie's Future*

Mother came to the big city of Bogalusa, Louisiana in 1943 for a one-night visit. She had one suitcase in hand and dreams for a bright tomorrow. She found work at the local U.S. Selective Service, commonly known as the draft board. It was there that she met Lahoma Clements, who befriended her and gave her room and board. That one night visit turned into 3 years and then a lifetime there in Bogalusa.

Lahoma had a cousin, Reggie Moak, who was in the Marines, and probably stationed in California. He was very handsome in his Marine uniform. What young girl could resist? A pen pal relationship ensued between Lennie and Reggie, which eventually lead to their courtship and marriage in 1945. As you can see, she is definitely smitten with him.

I was never privy to the reason they could not have children of their own. In late 1956, they adopted a chubby little baby boy, ME!

Mother reveled in telling all who would listen, that none of the clothes or shoes they had purchased for a six month old fit me upon arrival at my new home.

Many people over the years have shared with me how proud Lennie and Reggie were to have a baby boy in their family.

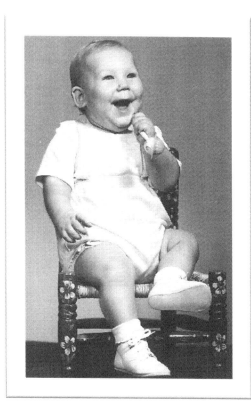

However, they must have felt that I needed company, because three years later, they adopted a baby girl, my new sister who they named Madonna. From all accounts, they loved us tremendously.

In 1961, however, the unthinkable happened. Just 5 years after adopting me, Reggie got sick and died from cirrhosis of the liver, contracted by tainted blood in transfusions.

Of Reggie, I only have a few memories. The first one I recall being maybe three or four years old. One Sunday after church, our pastor's son and I found our way to his room at the church parsonage, adjacent to the church. Toys, we just wanted to play with toys, while our parents were still talking and visiting with one another in the sanctuary.

In the late 50's or early 60's, there was no rush to be the first to arrive at the local restaurants for lunch like it is today. The pace of life was much slower then. Besides, most mothers prepared ahead, and Sunday dinner was eaten at home.

So, while our parents and others remained gathered in the sanctuary, we were hidden away in our little "toy world." By the time Reggie and Lennie were ready to go home, I was nowhere to be found.
I guess they looked for a long time before finding me because Reggie seemed very upset.

It was during the summer. I remember having short pants on, my chubby little legs exposed to the "swat, swat, swat" of a long switch that he had torn from a bush just to the left of the garage. I'm sure that I cried. Though it isn't a negative memory for me, I definitely remember that switching.

My other memory is that Reggie must have been in the hospital for some time, and maybe in his last days, he was brought to the house in an ambulance.

It was parked in the driveway, and I remember all the neighbors and family and friends taking turns leaning into the opened back door of the long Batman-looking vehicle with a red cherry light on top, each person taking a turn greeting him and wishing him well in his recovery. Those are my only two distinct memories of Reggie.

It's always been fun to have others share stories with me about my childhood. One Sunday afternoon, out of the blue, a longtime family friend, Betty Jo Sullivan Remel and a friend of hers stopped by the house for a visit. Neither Mother nor I had seen her in years.

What a wonderful time together. She and Mother talked of life and days gone by. It was a very happy "moment in time" that I shall always remember.

Betty Jo, with a "joie de vivre" that only she possessed, shared about the times she had baby sat for my sister and me and, about one particular Sunday morning in church, when apparently, I was really misbehaving.

Betty Jo said, "Greg, you were a bad little boy at times, and this morning in church you were so bad that your father took you by the hand and proceeded to walk you out of church." It was then that you started screaming at the top of your little lungs, "No, Daddy, no, Daddy. I'll be better Daddy, no, Daddy, no." I'm sure that everyone got a really big laugh that morning.

Not too long after her visit, John and Cheryl Douglas, Mother and I drove to Mize, MS, about an hour and half due north of Bogalusa, to attend Betty Jo's funeral. She was a victim of cancer. I'm so thankful that Betty Jo shared her story with Mother and me that Sunday afternoon.

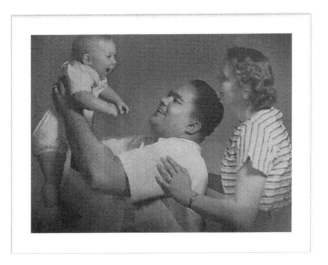

3   Over the Years

Mother's love for us was endless. She worked tirelessly at her job with the United Way, retiring in 1997 with 50 years of service. She always spoke fondly of Mr. A. R. Yates, who was her superior for forty-five of those fifty years.

After long days at work, she came home to prepare tasty meals. She helped with homework, but only if it didn't interrupt a ballgame, any game that might be on TV. That was my stubbornness.

I can never forget the way she lovingly mended the bumps and bruises from wrecks on my bicycle and the many strawberries on my knees and elbows from sliding in baseball games and practice, along with floor burns from basketball games played at the YMCA.

Let's not forget the loads and loads of laundry over the years that she did for us. From getting the blood stains out of all my uniforms to making sure that my go-to-church clothes were cleaned and ironed, she did it all.

She did all these things, and I'm sure many more. But, there was help along the way. Mrs. W. D. Finley, granny Finley, or "maw" Finley, as we affectionately called her was one of those special people. She lived just around the corner, in a small white cinder block home. Being so close was convenient. She stayed with us after school and all day during the summer months.

Maw Finley was a Godly woman and a smart one, too. One of her favorite words was "stickability." Is that actually a word? Lol. In our modern age of technology I just Googled stickability on my "smart phone" and, yes, it is a word. "A person's ability to persevere with something; staying power." Oh, how I wish I had heeded that one word of godly wisdom from her. She was so right!

But, I believe that the greatest way Mother showed her love was raising me in the church, our church, Westside Emmanuel Baptist. It was just 3 blocks from our house.

Though no one has ever point blank told me so, I'm almost positive Mother would have never made it after Reggie's death with a five-year old and a three-year old had it not been for the support of the church.

First Timothy 5:5 states, "A widow who is all alone, with no one to care for her, has placed her hope in God and continues to pray and ask Him for help day and night." (1 Timothy 5:5 GNT)

I truly believe Mother "placed her hope in God" and God's people, the members of Westside Emmanuel, answered. From the days spent in the cradle department until the day I graduated high school, I'm guessing that every time the doors of the church were open, we were there.

So, I am truly thankful that God, in His infinite wisdom, saw fit to bring, what was once, for whatever reason, a child unwanted, to an adoption, not only into the Moak family, but more importantly, into the family of God.

4   *Cake Maker*

Mother delighted in making cakes, candies and sweets. According to Mother, Reggie too enjoyed baking cakes.

One of Mother's joys in life was making birthday cakes for the ladies of Westside, who were 70 years of age and older. She had a long list, 25-50 members, who she made cakes for on their special day. Some claimed no one had ever made a cake for them. So, Mother enjoyed doing it, plus she had an opportunity to visit with them when she delivered the cake.

Somewhere along the way, Mother started making wedding cakes. She proudly made my sister, Madonna's, wedding cake. Mother's cakes were not so much known for how they looked, but how good they tasted. Everyone enjoyed eating Mother's cakes.

One of Mother's best neighbors over the years was Idelle McDonald. She also made wedding cakes, and she was very accomplished at decorating them. So, wanting to improve her skills, Mother spent many hours with Idelle learning from the best, how to decorate cakes.

Delivery of a birthday cake was a breeze. Birthday cakes were usually not so big, and could easily rest on the floor board or front seat of the car without too much worry. Or, a helper could ride along and hold the cake in their lap.

Wedding cakes, however, were a different matter. Some wedding cakes were about the same size as a birthday cake, and then some were comprised of multiple layers and sections, meaning transporting them became an issue. At least, for Mother, it did.

Mother had someone make a delivery aid made out of plywood. She probably found it in a cake-making magazine. It was about five and a half feet long by three feet wide and fit perfectly in the trunk of her car.

The board had three holes cut in it, a large hole in the center and two smaller holes on either side. The board was covered with soft foam that kept the cakes snuggly in place. With careful driving, there were usually no problems. Mother was very proud of her cake delivery board.

5   *Mother's BFFs*

Dorothy and Bolivar Sheridan, Ada Jones, Opal Sharp, Molly Hunt were some of the most special people to Mother. To my knowledge, these five people were Mother's closest and dearest friends, each, of course, for different reasons.

As a child, we visited the Sheridan's often. I knew them as Dorty and Bol. They lived in a shotgun house on Avenue C, just across the street from Pleasant Hill Elementary School. It was just six or eight blocks from our home in the 1100 block of Avenue J. Later in life they moved to a house on Avenue J just a few blocks from us.

Mother would tell visitors to Bogalusa that if you could count, and you knew your alphabet, getting around in Bogalusa was easy, as the north and south streets were alphabetic avenues and the east and west streets were numerical.

Dorty was kind and loving and always smiling. I can imagine that she and Mother were constantly trying new recipes, baking sugar cookies and loving on me.

Bolivar worked for Blue Cross Blue Shield Insurance. He was a deacon and Sunday school director at our church. He even taught me how to swim, sort of. It was in the Tangipahoa River near Ponchatoula, Louisiana one hot summer afternoon. Bol carried me out into the middle of the river, let go of me and said "swim." I did my best to dog paddle back to the shore so I guess you can say that was my first swimming lesson.

The January that my sister married was extremely cold, brutally cold for Bogalusa and the Deep South. The temperature was in the low teens and single digits as I recall.

Our home was built off the ground, meaning the water pipes were exposed to the elements. It doesn't take a genius to figure out there would be busted pipes to be replaced.

Bolivar and I took on the task of crawling under the house, bundled up in our warmest clothing. We found one pipe that definitely needed replacing. It was frigid cold, damp and muddy. What a mess! Being there was miserable. But, the job had to be done if we wanted running water. We had been without water for several days, and Mother had a pile of dishes in the sink that she wanted cleaned and put away.

As we were crawling out with the dismantled pipe in hand, I noticed another pipe that would also need replacing. I pointed right at the problem, but Bol couldn't see it. He was the adult in charge, so if he couldn't see it, then there was nothing to worry about.

After a trip to J.K. Hardware to get a new pipe measured and threaded, it was back to the frozen quagmire beneath the house. Finally, success! With the new pipe in place and the water main turned back on there was... there was another burst pipe, the one that I had pointed out to Bol earlier. The one he did not see.

Though freezing wet, muddy and tired from this little adventure, and knowing another trip to the hardware store and back would follow, I still had a wry smile knowing that I was right and he was wrong. Or, at least that my eyesight was better.

Over the years, we laughed many times as that experience came up in conversation. But, I can assure you that I was not laughing on that brutally cold and miserable day many years ago.

Dorty and Bol died within 4 months of one another, and are buried just yards from Mother at Hillview Memorial Gardens, just outside of Bogalusa on Spring Valley Road.

I loved so much Brother Bennie Jones, and still love his wife, Mrs. Ada. They had two daughters, Brenda and Glenda and two sons, James and Eddie who were close in age with me. We went to church together and with many of our neighborhood friends, we played football and baseball in Bennie and Ada's big yard.

When I think of the friendship that was forged between Mother and Mrs. Ada, I'm sure it was bonded and secured right there at Westside Emmanuel Church. A God thing!

While caring for Mother, I resigned myself to doing many things I never ever imagined doing. I had to help her dress and undress, get her into and out of the tub, and help her with bathing. I washed her hair, helped her into and out of bed, her wheel chair, and the car.

You get the picture. I lovingly and willingly helped her in many ways BUT the ONE thing I would NOT DO, no way and no how, was to roll her hair! I had no problem washing her hair, but I refused to roll it, PERIOD!

Fortunately, Mrs. Ada would come to the house where she and Mom would enjoy visiting, while the retired beautician would roll her hair. Later, when Ada didn't drive so much, I would wash Mother's hair, and then take her the two blocks to Ada's house. Their visits, our visits, were always so relaxed and special. I didn't fully realize, until after Mother's death, how close she and Ada were.

Before leaving Bogalusa, I shared lunch with Mrs. Ada one day, and she told me how much she missed Mother and that she never had such a close friend as Lennie. Losing Lennie, she said was one of the toughest things she ever had to deal with. You will always be special to me Mrs. Ada Jones.

Mrs. Opal Sharp was my kindergarten teacher. She ran her kindergarten out of her home, which had a large yard for playing games. It was located just one street over, and four and a half blocks from our house.

She was a pillar in the church, never one for lack of words, and she loved her family and church. I believe she and Mother loved each other dearly.

They would often take trips together to visit each other's families in Franklinton or in Mississippi. Later in life, when Mrs. Opal was in an assisted living facility, just off north Columbia Street in Bogalusa, I would take Mother there for many visits. They just enjoyed being together. Now they are together again in eternity, treading the streets of gold.

Molly and Jack Hunt were an interesting couple. They lived right across the street from the church. Like so many others, I'm sure the church is where their friendship with my Mother was born.

Over the years, I remember going to their home with Mom. She and Mrs. Molly would drink coffee inside, while Mr. Jack and I would sit out in the back yard in the swing and 'shoot the breeze.' After Molly's death, Mother spoke of their visits, and enjoying many cups of coffee and hours of idle chat.

Tonya Magee, now Tonya Magee Keaton, though not one of Mother's BFFs, was certainly one of my BFFs. We met, where else, but at church, and soon became good friends and walking buddies. Tonya loves people and has a servant heart. She immediately took a liking to Mother.

Numerous times, Tonya would give me a break and keep Mother, often spoiling her with baths, washing, rolling, and drying her hair, and giving her manicures. I know that Mother thoroughly enjoyed these times with Tonya. What woman doesn't like being totally spoiled? If Tonya didn't cook while at the house, she always brought food with her. Most of the time, she would bring her little sister Madison, too.

I would be remiss if I didn't mention all of the 'angels' who offered a respite for me. Besides the companionship they gave to Mother, being able to provide me with four or five hours, one day a week to get away, was invaluable.

So I say THANK YOU and GOD BLESS to: Karla and Katie Mizell, Debbie Wadley Kinzle, Bonnie Cothern, Mildred Crockett, Mary McBeth, Lamar and Mary Bryan, Faye Jenkins, Mrs. Sylvia Lambert, Sarah Stewart, Ada Jones, Gladys Alford, Beverly Brady, Mrs.Doris Byrd, Alton Byrd, my cousin Martha Moak, and my cousin Kim Lewis. If I have left someone's name out, please forgive me.

6   *My Childhood Memories*

Mother worked hard to provide for my sister and me. We were indeed blessed. We got almost everything we ever asked for, especially on birthdays and at Christmas.

My grandmother, Lucille Purvis, Reggie's mother, was of great assistance helping Mother provide my sister and me with not only great things, but greater memories.

I was a sports fanatic, even at an early age. One Christmas, I desperately wanted a football but not just any football. I wanted a genuine, certified NFL football. I was the happiest kid around after opening that gift. I asked for it, and that's what I got - an NFL football.

My grandmother, who I called Maw Maw, lived across town on Sabine Street. Across town in Bogalusa meant a five minute drive.

I loved going to Maw Maw's. Like most grandmothers, she did her best to spoil me. I know she did things for my sister as well, but it seemed that I was the one constantly at her home, always there with her.

She loved to cook and made many wonderful meals, especially every other Sunday, when my uncle, Reggie's brother Lindrose, and his wife, Alice, would be there, along with their Chihuahua dog, always a fat and well-fed little doggie. They would arrive at my grandmother's mid-afternoon on Saturdays, and then leave late afternoon on Sundays, heading back to their home in Mobile.

One of her favorite Sunday meals to prepare was spaghetti and meatballs with homemade sauce and garlic French bread. Not being a pasta lover, I only ate the meatballs, sauce and bread. Maw Maw also made a tasty 'from scratch' pizza.

Mother enjoyed telling a joke about a young bride with her grocery list, scurrying up and down the aisles of the local supermarket. After seeing a panicked look on her face, the market manager asked if he could be of assistance. To which the young bride replied, "I've been looking, and looking, but just can't find the SCRATCH."

I enjoyed many Friday and Saturday night sleepovers at my grandmother's. She was warm, loving, and proper. Her sense of being proper was evidenced the night I got excited watching a football game, and in my excitement, I let out a big fart. With much laughter, I exclaimed, "Maw Maw, I farted." To which she replied, "No Greg, you must always say "passed gas"."

My first dog was a German Shepherd which was bought for me by my grandmother. I was in elementary school, and I'm not sure if she discussed the idea with my mother, but we all adapted. It was a good dog and great pet.

One day I came home from school and there was no barking or excited dog to greet me. I somehow instinctively knew that he was gone. He was, gone to doggie heaven, a victim of heart worms.

Family vacations are always special. I don't recall every one of ours, but one that sticks out in my mind was the trip to Six Flags Over Texas, making the five-hundred mile journey from Bogalusa to Arlington in a green and white '56 or '57 Chevy. Mother did all the driving, with Aunt Bessie riding shotgun, with my sister and me in the back seat.

It was a fun trip. We had a great time at Six Flags riding all the rides, and, of course, swimming at the hotel pool. It was all so much fun.

Mother always made sure that my birthday parties were special. I'm sure in the very early years it was cake and ice cream with family. But, as I got into late elementary years, the parties became all about me and my friends. Most parties, weather permitting, were held or started in the back yard.

At one particular party, the main attraction was not busting open a piñata, but two guys busting open one another's face. A fight broke out at my party; a bloody one at that. I am not sure what started it, but thank goodness, it was over quickly. I'm pretty sure Mother did not pre-arrange that fiasco.

May 13, my birthday, usually coincided with the summer opening of the swimming pool at the local YMCA. So Mother would buy one-day passes for all at my party to go swimming, and that's usually where the party ended.

A summer-long swimming pass was usually one of my customary gifts. If not in the Y pool, I was usually playing ping pong. Yes, Kenny, I know it's TABLE TENNIS, but growing up, it was ping pong. I loved learning and playing that game.

The director of the Y, Mr. Gay, was an excellent player, along with a man named Mr. Haik. They would beat me mercilessly, but it was a great learning experience that made me a better player in the long run.

One of my all-time favorite Christmas gifts was a ping pong table. I could never figure out how Santa Claus got that table into our living room!

Over the years, many people have asked, "How did you get the nickname "Granny"?" Mr. T.A. Byrd, one of my little league coaches, gave it to me by accident, I suppose and it stuck.

Baseball practice at Denhamtown Elementary School diamond was almost over. Everyone had gathered at home plate, but me. I was playing third base, and was the last one to have my in-field practice ball hit to me.

Instead of a hard hit ground ball, Mr. Byrd intentionally hit the ball over my head into left field. He then shouted, "Run, go get that ball, Gregory." Well off I went, running as fast as I could run. After just a few strides, I could hear the coaches and my team mates laughing and carrying on around the backstop. So I decided if they were having fun at my expense, then I wasn't going to 'run' after the ball.

When my run became a walk, it was then that Coach Byrd looked out at me and proclaimed, "Is that as fast as you can run? You run like an old granny." The rest, as they say, is HISTORY!

Being raised in the church, Westside Emmanuel Baptist Church, it was only fitting that from a very early age I attended VBS, Vacation Bible School.

During the cleanup process of Mother's home I found a VBS group photo taken on the front steps of the church. It was in remarkable condition, considering the fact that it was in a rusty filing cabinet on the back porch. Who knows when that filing cabinet had last been opened?

Amazingly, almost everyone in the photo, and there were approximately 200 or more adults and children, did a great job of looking into the camera. Some had smiles and some not.

Out of curiosity, I posted the picture online at a link on Facebook called "Bogalusa Then and Now." It proved to have great interest, not only with those who were in the picture, but among all who viewed it. Many enjoyed trying to figure out who was who.

The greatest decision I've ever made, or will ever make, was to give my life to Jesus Christ. It was in VBS at Westside when I was 12 years old that I made that commitment. Thank you, Brother Lawrence Baylot, our pastor at the time, for leading me and countless others to saving grace.

Of the three main team sports, baseball, football and basketball, baseball was my first love. I've told many people over the years that my scholastic endeavors suffered greatly, through no one's fault but my own, because I was given a plastic ball and bat as a gift in my early years.

WIKC, a local radio station, was the sponsor of a nationwide contest where you threw the ball for distance, at a target for accuracy, and then ran the bases as fast as you could run. I won in my age bracket, and was awarded an all-expense- paid trip to Houston, TX to compete against kids from all over the United States inside the 8th Wonder of the World, the Astrodome.

One of several cool things about winning the trip was wearing an Astros replica uniform, while competing and staying at the Shamrock Hilton Hotel in downtown Houston. It's also where the visiting pro teams playing the Astros would stay. That weekend the Astro's were playing the San Francisco Giants.

The Giants had many good players, including the great Willie Mays and, familiar names known to most all true baseball fans. Team mates included Willie McCovey, Juan Marichal, Orlando Cepeda, Gaylord Perry, Jim Davenport, Hal Lanier, Jesus Alou, and Bobby Bonds.

I was fortunate to get Willie Mays, Juan Marichal, Willie McCovey and Orlando Cepeda's autographs on my playing glove. What a thrill!

Over the years, the way autograph and sports memorabilia has evolved, can you imagine what that glove might be worth today?

Back then, I had no idea about autograph collecting and its possible future profitability. The reality is, and don't all you autograph collectors cringe, like a young boy with only one glove would do, yes, even that glove with those four autographs, I returned home and continued playing ball with it, taking ground and fly balls with it, throwing it into the dugout between innings, yes probably on the ground. Heck, one of my dogs probably chewed on it at some point. Yes, now, all four of those Giant players are in the Hall of Fame.

My favorite band while in early high school years, the first band I ever saw in live concert, was Three Dog Night. The concert was in Jackson, MS. My best friend, Bruce Ballard, and I were very excited to have the opportunity to see them on stage in a live performance.

I'm sure that we rocked the night away listening to all their great hits, but the one thing that grabbed my attention more so than the concert itself, was the fringed moccasin boots that the drummer Floyd Sneed was wearing. Man, they were so cool. I just could not get those fringed moccasin boots out of my mind.

In the days and weeks after the concert, my mother and I searched high and low for a pair of those cool fringed moccasin boots and, finally,

finally we found them. It was in New Orleans. I don't remember the name of the store, but YES, finally I had my pair of moccasins with the fringe on top.

There was just one little problem. I didn't look nearly as cool wearing them as did the drummer for Three Dog Night. All that excitement, all that searching, and I didn't wear those fringed moccasin boots more than a couple of times.

While I wanted to share a little background information about Mother and me, the rest of these pages tell of our love for each other over the last 6 years and 20 days of her life.

7   May 4th 2007

I left Orlando, Florida on May 4th, 2007 and arrived back in Bogalusa at 1113 Avenue J, the home and address where I was raised, and where my mother still lived. I was in the process of getting a divorce. Mother would say, "I hate that Greg's marriage didn't work out, but I am sure glad to have him home with me."

Mother's doctor had been telling me for several years that she should not be living alone. Besides her diabetes, Mother was fairly healthy. Dr. B as Mother referred to him, called it "that Wascom disease." My guess is he doctored Aunt Iris, Uncle T.J., Uncle Clyde, as well as Mother, all of whom were diabetic.

I never knew Mother to be sick, or to have spent any time in a hospital. She would say that she was one of those "disgustingly healthy people." In the later days of my stay with her, after multiple trips to the ER and stays in different hospitals and long term care, it was payback time for being so disgustingly healthy all her life.

She was blessed and I was happy that she had excellent insurance coverage. So, it was only natural for me because of my love for her to come home and care for her.

8   *Encouraging Words*

From the moment I arrived home, until Mother's death and even beyond, I've been amazed at the number of people, especially total strangers, who would come up to me and say, "God is going to bless you for what you are doing."

As we were out and about doing our normal activities, for as long as Mother could go, they would see me assisting her, caring for her, holding her upright, pushing her in her wheelchair, doing all the things that a caregiver does to care for their patient. Some would ask if that was my mother. Others knew I was her son.

As much as those words and those people would encourage me, it has been perplexing to try and understand just exactly what this blessing is, and when is it going to occur.

Has the blessing already occurred, as I cared for her? Is this blessing going to occur in my lifetime? Will it not take place till I am in eternity with Jesus? These questions have passed through my mind ever since I first heard that God was going to bless me.

The fifth commandment says, "Honor thy father and Mother that thy days may be long upon the land which the Lord thy God giveth thee." (Exodus 20:12 KJV). It is also the first commandment with a promise.

As I previously stated, I loved my mother tremendously. It was an honor to be with her and care for her in her last years, days, and moments. For me, it was the right thing to do. So, it was out of this tremendous love and respect for her that I counted it all JOY to be her caregiver. It was most important for me to be a loving son who felt compassion for her and her needs long before I ever heard the words, "God is going to bless you."

I have said that my life may never amount to anything that is important, at least important in worldly standards, but if I never do anything extraordinary in this life, I do believe that caring for my mother was the most important thing that I shall ever accomplish.

9   *Years of Loneliness*

When I think of all the years Mother spent alone, it amazes me. People endure loneliness for many reasons. I got a good look at loneliness the year after Mother's death, and to some degree, even now. In Mother's case, at least part of her being lonely was due to her sacrifice for my sister and me.

I remember a man named Emmett Corkern. I'm not really sure how he and Mother met, or when he started coming to the house for visits. He was a nice, polite man. He wore a hat, I guess because of his balding on top, I don't really know. But wearing a hat suited Emmett.

He shared meals with us. From time to time he would go on trips with us to visit family. We went to Hattiesburg, MS a time or two to Mack's Fish Camp to eat. I was very unsuspecting of Emmett.

One night, like many others, Emmett came for a visit. When he was ready to leave, he and Mother went out the back door, closed it behind them, and stood on the back steps talking.

The den window, which faced the back of the house and was just a few feet away from the back steps, was open, and like a curious young boy, I was listening to their every word. When it suddenly got quiet, I wondered what they could be doing. So, I peeped out the window, and to my shock and surprise, they were embracing one another and kissing.

They were both single and lonely. I'm sure that hugging and kissing was natural for them. But, I can tell you for a young impressionable boy who had never seen his mother kiss anyone other than Reggie, it was confusing and I cried.

When Emmett left and Mother came back inside, she could see that I was crying, and wanted to know what was wrong. I told her that I had seen her and Emmett kissing. WHY? I am not 100% sure, but I would be willing to bet they never kissed again, and if they did, it was somewhere that I had no possibility of seeing them. Emmett died in 1994.

Although someone once mentioned to me there was a rumor that Mother had been involved with someone else after Emmett's death, though possible, I highly doubt it. I do remember asking her one time why she never remarried. Her answer was, "If someone could not put you and your sister before anything else, she would rather stay single."

Now that's sacrificial love.

10   Sign of Things to Come

The summer of 2007 was just like many others. Mother was mobile, and able to go and do things without much difficulty. She was still driving.

Mrs. Mildred Crockett, a friend and neighbor of Mother's who lived just three houses down the street, they would share turns driving themselves to the Senior Center, located at the north end of Ave F and on the outskirts of Cassidy Park. It was there they enjoyed fellowship with other seniors and a $1.00 meal.

Once a month they would get up before the crack of dawn to drive about a mile or so and queue up to receive their FREE groceries given by the Catholic Charities out of New Orleans.

Though Mother could drive, I preferred to drive whenever we went anywhere. It was only natural that I do so. Mother just accepted it, and at some point along the way, she just ceased driving.

I had heard stories of transitioning parents away from driving. Those car keys I'm sure are the last connection to independence for some. Because I was home with Mother, and I drove everywhere, that transition for us was not a problem. Still, there were many times I would hear Mother say to others, "I can still drive!"

In reality, she could, but not so well. In fact, her driving skills had been diminishing for some time. Several years ago, Mother had experienced squirrels chewing on power lines leading into the house causing the loss of a TV, microwave, and various outlet problems that needed an electrician. On the day that the electrician arrived, I was in the back yard washing my vehicle. Mother showed the electrician the problems that needed repairing, and then lickety-split, she was out the back door and headed to her car parked in the garage. "Mom, where are you going?" "I need to run a few errands", was her reply. I said, "Why don't you wait until the repairman is finished?" She said he is OK, and she needed to get some things done. OK.

I continued washing my car as she started her engine and proceeded to back up and out the long driveway onto the street. BANG! I heard this loud noise and immediately knew that Mom had backed right into the electrician's little red pick-up truck parked at the end of the drive.

I went running and opened the driver's side door to Mom's car. "Mom, are you ok?" "Yes." "Mom, didn't you see the red truck in the drive?" "No", she said. "Oh, Mom!" Then she asked, "Haven't you ever made a mistake? Let it go, Greg. No one is hurt, and damage to either vehicle is very minor." As I said, the transition of taking the keys away went smoothly for us.

11   *Sister Visits*

Mother constantly talked about wanting to see Madonna, the grandchildren, and the great grand-children. Madonna and her husband, David, live in Pumpkin Center, where they are close to their son, Joshua, and his wife, April, and their two grandchildren, Ava and Lilly. But, for Mother to see them, it was necessary to take her on a two-hour drive, one hour going and one hour coming home. For some reason, my sister seldom made the trip to Mother's house.

Mother's granddaughter, Carlie, lives in the Baton Rouge area, about a fifty-minute drive away from Pumpkin Center. Unless there was a special occasion, we didn't always see Carlie.

In the first few years of making the trip to Madonna's it wasn't an issue for Mom or me, but as Mother's health declined, it did become an issue for me that never really got resolved.

As time went by, and Mother's dementia progressed, there would be moments, especially late in the evening, when we were leaving my sister's house that Mother swore we were leaving someone behind. I believe it's referred to as 'sun downing' – 'confusion and agitation as the sun goes down, and sometimes through the night.'

I would do my best to keep a calm voice, and explain to her that it was just she and I who had made the trip. To explain where we had just been, and who it was we had visited.

One time, she cried because she knew we were leaving someone behind, and that I needed to turn around and go back after them. She couldn't figure out who it was. I sensed her frustration of not understanding. There was frustration on my behalf also. Having patience really is a virtue.

12   Doing What You Have To Do

Over the six years of caring for Mother, of course her condition changed, and our approach and solution to each issue came about mainly out of necessity.

Mother was never embarrassed or shy about the fact that her grown son was helping her dress or bathe. I believe she was more than happy that it was me, and not some total stranger.

In the beginning, once I got her into the tub, she was able to bathe herself and then call me when she was ready to be helped out. Later, I helped wash her back, and sometimes we washed her hair while she was in the tub, but when that became too difficult, we washed her hair as she would stand in front of the kitchen sink. It was just easier for both of us.

In the beginning, after bathing, she was able to dry herself, but when the time came, she didn't mind at all that I would dry her whole body off. I assisted her into her nightgown and then helped her into bed. We did what we had to do.

For the first two or three years after coming home, I slept in my old bedroom. If Mother needed me during the night, she would just call for me.

The main reason she would call, is for assistance to the bathroom and then right back into bed. But, somewhere along the way, she stopped calling for me, and I would be awakened by a crashing noise, the sound of her body hitting the floor and her crying out for help.

No matter how late I waited to go to bed myself, I never seemed to get a good night's sleep. Though I've never had a new born baby to care for, I'm sure, in ways, this was similar; always listening, always thinking, "What next?"

After multiple times of her getting out of bed and falling, I made the decision to buy a set of baby monitors. Sneaky huh! May I say, those monitors worked very well. I could hear her every breath if I listened closely enough and I was easily alerted to her calls for me, or to her attempts to crawl out of bed on her own. Problem solved. Or, so I thought.

There were nights that I would be so tired that I found myself in such a deep sleep that she would make her way out of bed and to the bathroom, or had fallen before I heard anything.

Even with the baby monitor, she was continuing to get out of bed during the night, sometimes falling, sometimes not. I had another decision to make.

After much thought, and a few talks with close friends, I made the decision that would work best for us, and that was for me to sleep in the bed with her. It was a king-size bed, plenty of room for us to have our own space. Since I would be sleeping on the open side of the bed, the side not hemmed in by a wall, she would literally have to crawl over me if she needed or wanted to get out of bed.

As strange as it may seem, a grown man sleeping in the same bed as his mother, this was the best possible solution for us. It worked. When she needed to get up, she just told me so, no calling across the house, and I would help her up and out of bed and to the toilet and back. NO MORE FALLING.

Several funny things about being in the same bed with Mother. Even though it was a big bed with our own space, her dementia was now taking a toll on her, and I am positive that many times she thought that I was her husband, Reggie.

With my back to her, she did enjoy snuggling up to me and putting her arm over my side. I would hold her hand against my chest, and I know this made her feel secure and comforted.

13 *Broken Ribs*

Mother looked forward to visiting with her brother, Clyde. It was just a thirty minute drive from our house to his house on Main St. in Franklinton. They were both happy to spend time together, though our visits usually didn't last very long.

On one trip, we had just pulled into the driveway. Mother was waiting in her seat while I opened her Rollator, a combo walker and chair on wheels. It was now opened, and I helped her out of the Durango, and off she went. But, only a few steps away, and just behind the vehicle, out of my sight, she lost her balance.

She had issues with her fluctuating blood pressure, so my guess is that she got dizzy and started falling. She wasn't strong enough to hold herself up, or quick enough to realize her dizziness, and just sit down in the chair.

The fall happened so quickly. As I took a few steps to where she was, I could see the last moment of her hitting the concrete, falling on top of her Rollator. I knew it had to hurt. Helping her to her feet, it was evident that she was in pain. It was her belly and side that hurt.

A day later, it was apparent that the pain was not going away, so we made a visit to Dr. B. The x-rays confirmed the source of the pain; three broken ribs. No wonder her pain wasn't going away.

14   The Beginning of the End

Dr. B used to tell Mom all the time that if she fell and broke her hip, it would be the beginning of the end. But, I truly believe that for my mother, the beginning of her end began with a terrible cough just before Christmas 2012. Due to this constant coughing, we made a trip to the local ER, where she was admitted with bronchitis.

After a few nights of antibiotics and care, she was released, and we came home. Christmas came and went, but the persistence of the coughing did not go away. I knew she was going to need specialized attention, so off we went to the ER at St. Tammany Hospital in Covington, about a forty minute drive from our house.

After hours in the ER, she was admitted with pneumonia. Again, her stay was filled with many treatments of antibiotics. Admitted on the 2nd of January 2013, and released on the 7th of January, the doctors highly suggested continued antibiotic treatments via transfusion at a long-term care facility. Fortunately, there was such a facility in Bogalusa. After consulting with the staff and upon knowledge of an available bed, we left St. Tammany Hospital and drove straight to the long-term acute care facility located in the old Calvary Baptist Church on south Columbia Street.

Upon arrival, and with just a little paperwork for me to sign, Mother was quickly resting in her new home away from home, which is where she would be recovering for the next twenty-three days. In the beginning, I would stay with her during the night to help keep her comfortable and calm. Then, I would leave around 5 am to go home and get a little rest for myself. I would return around 11:30 am to help feed her, and I would stay until mid-afternoon.

Hopefully, she would be asleep, and I would sneak away until I returned to keep her company until she fell asleep for the night. That cycle went on for a week, or so. I soon was able to stay away more and more and leave her for the night earlier and earlier, but that didn't mean she liked it.

There was a handful of times that the medical staff would call me, day and night, and ask if I would come back to help calm her anxiety.

Throughout her stay, she just couldn't understand why she, why we, couldn't just go home! By the last days of her stay, I was wondering the same thing.

15   Broken Hip?

We were back home again from seemingly continuous hospital stays and the 23 days of long term care for a couple of weeks. Mom was in bed, resting, sleeping most of this particular day, weak and fragile as she continued recovering from pneumonia.

Beverly, a neighbor and classmate, had offered to help with Mother whenever needed so I called to see if she might be able to stay with her while l went grocery shopping. She was able to help and came right over.

Mother was still sleeping, so off I went. I didn't need much, so I was finished and loading the groceries into the Durango in a flash. As I pulled out of the parking lot on my way back home I decided to call Beverly to see how things were going and to let her know I was on my way home.

Beverly had just looked in on her for a second time and found her on the floor. Mother was in some pain but Beverly said she would wait until I arrived to get her back in bed. This was typical of Mother to be resting one moment and then be on the move the next. Expect the unexpected. When I knelt by her side to raise her up it was evident that she was in great pain around her waist. We managed to get her back into bed as gently as possible.

In my heart I knew that she had finally broken her hip. Thinking that we needed professional assistance I called 911 and before too long paramedics were there checking her out, finally deciding that she should be examined by a doctor.

The paramedics transported Mother and I arrived only minutes later at the local ER. After several hours the results from x-rays had been read. She did not have a broken hip but a broken right pelvic bone. For me, this was just as bad as a broken hip. No need for surgery, it would heal in time on its own.

This was not a very good gift. Her 89th birthday was coming soon and for the next couple of months she would have to rely on pain meds and lots of rest as she recovered.

It was now time for hospice care. Most people associate hospice as being "'in the last days" when in fact, according to our hospice nurse, Larry, hospice care can be with a patient for a year or more and in some instances the patient will improve somewhat as opposed to a steady decline toward death. I could see and understand that reasoning but in Mother's case I had no positive thoughts of that being a reality for us.

Mother's pelvic bone did finally heal. The pain finally went away and oddly enough she even preferred sleeping on her right side.

16 Choking Episodes

About a month or so before Mother's death, I was still attempting to feed her solid food. She was eating very little at this time and I wanted to do my best to keep her satisfied and nourished. Hospice had replaced Mother's nice king size bed with a new hospital bed that could be raised and lowered with the touch of a button.

This particular day I had her sitting up at about a 60 degree angle. She had just begun eating when she started coughing. It was nothing out of the ordinary. Many times in the past she had trouble swallowing, a sort of gagging, but it would always clear and she could swallow her food.

I encouraged her to take a sip of juice. I patted her on the back lightly but it quickly became evident that she was not going to be able to swallow. She was now blue in the face and limp. I cleared her tray and lowered her bed as I positioned myself behind her to start the Heimlich maneuver, which I had never done before.

I remember saying out loud, "Oh Lord no, please don't take her like this. We have been through so much, not like this Lord."

Being forceful but gentle I began the thrust of my balled fist inward and upward, doing my best to force the lodged food from her throat. My adrenaline was sky high. My mother's tiny body and life were in my arms but I had a calm assurance, knowing and believing that GOD was in total control.

FINALLY the food was dislodged. If there was a cork popping sound as the food cleared her passage way I did not hear it. Color returned to her face and she was no longer in distress. WOW! That was very scary.

About 2 weeks later, she was resting on the couch in the den. While eating lunch, she began choking, AGAIN! This time it was not as severe, the gagging stopped and the food was quickly cleared. The Heimlich maneuver was not needed. But it was the last time that I gave her any form of solid food. Mother never drank much water but from that day forward water and different juices and squeezable smoothies would be all she would get.

17   *Always a Mother*

Back in 1992, when I moved to Orlando, Florida to start work at a certain "house owned by a mouse", I experienced my first migraine headache. It was really strange. Until that time, I couldn't recall having many regular headaches.

Over the last 20 years, I've had maybe ten migraines, which I don't consider to be many. I have compassion for those who have them daily, or even weekly or monthly. There were two times while caring for Mother that I had really bad migraines. One night while watching TV in the den, I felt a headache coming on. It was about 9:30 pm. Mother had been in bed asleep for over an hour. I took my usual 1,000 mg of Tylenol hoping to halt the headache from becoming a migraine.

Two hours later, no luck. My head is still pounding. By now I've turned off the TV and the lights and I am sitting in the dark, motionless, praying that it will go away real soon. If I can just make my way over to the couch, lie down, and fall asleep, maybe that will help.

Getting out of the chair seemed like I was moving in slow motion. For those of you who suffer from migraines, you totally understand. Sliding out of the recliner onto my knees, my all four's, I crawled the three feet to the couch. Once there and feeling very nauseous, I rested the side of my face on the couch, trying to muster the energy to get the rest of my body off the floor.

All of a sudden, I noticed that Mother was standing in the doorway leading out of her bedroom. "Oh, great", I'm thinking. I have a massive migraine and now I have to deal with Mother. I said, "Mom, please go back to bed." With her blood pressure issues, I knew that she could fall at any moment. "Mom, please at least sit down. I don't want you to fall." Of course, she wants to know what's wrong. I tell her I'm not feeling well but that I will be OK soon. One last time I beg her to go back to bed. The pain is so bad that I can barely keep my eyes open.

Faintly, I see that she is still in the doorway. By the time I reopen my eyes again, my mother is sitting on the floor next to me. She put one arm over one of my shoulders and then rested her head on the backside of my other shoulder. She was loving me and helping me the only way that she knew how.

On another night, I experienced a second migraine. It too came late at night after Mother was already asleep. I took my 1,000 mg of Tylenol and even contemplated taking another 500 mg tablet.

Somehow I knew that this was going to be a very serious migraine; so serious that I instinctively knew I would need medical assistance at the ER of the local hospital.

I had never needed a doctor's attention for my migraines, but this time was different. The medicine and a dark and quiet place were just not going to be enough. But, I wasn't going to leave without telling Mother. For her to wake and me not be there would be disastrous.

It was after 11 pm when I woke her, telling her that I needed to go to the ER. I assured her that because of the late hour, I felt confident that I would be treated and back home in about 2 hours. Of course, she wanted to go with me. "But why, Mother? You are comfortably in bed, and there is no need for you to go." If she only knew how badly my head was hurting and realized the effort it would take in my condition to get her out of bed, dressed, into her wheel chair and into the Durango. But, she didn't know or realize, and I quickly understood there was only going to be one outcome here, so off we go to the hospital.

It's after midnight, and though Mother and I are in an examining room, I still have not seen a doctor yet and Mom is constantly asking me, "How are you, and are you feeling better?"

I needed and wanted a shot to make the pain go away. Finally, a doctor came in, and a shot was given, but only after I agreed not to drive back home. Now what?

Mary McBeth, a close friend, who has helped care for Mother, once told me that many nights she didn't sleep well, and would read until the early morning hours. She lived only blocks from the hospital. I prayed, and took a chance that at 2:30 am I would not be waking her.

I was so happy and relieved to hear her voice, not sounding as if she had been in a long and deep sleep. She picked us up about 30 minutes later. The shot had started its good works by then and I was able to sleep until mid-morning. Once again, even in her condition, she had been the best mother she knew how to be.

18 *Last Getaway or Did I Make a Mistake*

Over the course of the six years and twenty days that I was caring for my mother, twenty-four hours a day, seven days a week, I was blessed beyond measure to have some wonderful friends who would come and relieve me, give me a partial day off, or to do whatever. That whatever was almost always golf with my senior buddies, Gary Hall, John Douglas, Bobby Speights, W. T. Amacker, Woodrow Hobgood, and many others.

There were times, depending on Mother's condition that I might not even get that one half-day away. My sister would also keep Mother at her house for a night or a long weekend to allow me to get away. I am eternally, physically and emotionally, grateful to all.

Not long before Mother's passing, I made a trip to visit Keri and Darlene Breland in Denham Springs. My friendship with Keri goes way back. He is also from Bogalusa, and I was a groomsman in his wedding. Anytime I visited in the Baton Rouge area and stayed overnight, it was usually with him. Our ping pong battles at his mother's house in Bogalusa were epic. He was a lefty and I was a righty. We would play for hours. We were ping pong legends in our own minds.

Mother had become very weak and was on oxygen by this time. I was exhausted and knew that I needed a break. We were on their patio enjoying some fresh boiled crayfish and all the accoutrements. It was a beautiful day with wonderful friends. Then it hit me. Did I make a mistake leaving her? She could die at any moment, and I wouldn't be there.

Anytime I was gone away from her for any length of time, she always wanted to know where I was and when I would be getting back home. When I did return, she always greeted me with open arms, reaching out to me for a big hug.

As we were eating those mudbugs, pinching da tails and sucking da heads, it's a Loooooooooziana thing, I thought of her reaching out to me as she always did, and for a brief moment, I choked up and thought that I should get up and go straight back to her. But I realized my need to totally trust God in all things and all situations and I understood my need to rest.

My silent prayer was, "Lord, let me see her open arms reaching out to me just one more time."

19   *Systems Shutdown*

One day in early May of 2013, I realized that Mother had not urinated in almost twelve hours. After consulting with the hospice nurse, Larry, he concluded that her kidneys were shutting down and that she may only have two to four days left. He suggested that I call family members.

So that's what I did. In the next couple of days, family, friends, and pastoral staff all came by for visits. While my sister was visiting, I decided to get away and try to get my mind off of everything that was going on and what was likely to happen.

My friend, Gary Hall, wanted to play golf, so we went to Millbrook Golf Course in Picayune, MS. It was less than an hour away should I need to return home on short notice.

While on the golf course, in the middle of our round of golf, I got the same feeling that I had that day eating those crayfish at Keri's. Did I make a mistake by leaving?" Again my prayer was, "Lord, let me see her open arms reaching out to me just ONE MORE TIME."

After our round of golf was completed and we were back inside the Bogalusa city limits, my cell phone rang and I could see it was my sister's cell number. Was this THE CALL?

"Hi, Madonna," I said. She replied, "Where are you? We are passing the Post Office." She then said that Mother wanted to talk with me. My mother wanted to talk with me! I had such a huge smile knowing she was still alive.

"Greg, where are you? Hurry home." She wanted me home. She always wanted me home. Again, God blessed me with answered prayer. To see those arms of hers reaching out to give and to get a great big hug, one more time.

Had her kidneys shut down? NO! It wasn't long after the incorrect diagnosis on her kidneys that her blood pressure dropped dramatically. Larry again suspected the end to be near, within 24 to 48 hours.

Now all of this was taking place close to Mother's Day and my birthday, the 12th and 13th respectively. So, I am thinking, "Great, she is really going to make her departure memorable." But, those days came and went, and she was still holding on; very weak, seemingly skin and bones, but holding on, none the less.

20 Tell Her It's OK to Go?

A friend of ours, Bonnie Montero Cothern, who had been a member at Westside Emmanuel in the past, and has known Mother and me for a very long time, told me on several occasions that I needed to tell my mother it was OKAY for her to go to Heaven, to be with Jesus, and that I would be okay.

Others had also said the same. Now, I've heard that before; people telling loved ones that it's okay to GO ON, to be at peace. It makes sense to me. But now I am wondering, why do I have to tell my mother that it's okay for her to "'let go of life"? WHY?

I thought about it, and one night late, when I could not sleep, I turned on some soothing hymnal music and sat on her bedside holding her hand. She was resting comfortably with her oxygen. I don't know if she knew it was me. I hoped that she would at least be able to hear me. Before I knew it, I was bawling my eyes out while trying to tell her it was okay for her to go be with Jesus, and that I would be okay.

Soon I had composed myself, and said what I had to say. I felt some personal relief. I gave her my permission. So, I turned out the small light above the bed, and slipped back into the recliner chair. Some days later I saw Bonnie, and told her what I had done.

I'm thinking that she is going to be proud that I did what she said I needed to do, and then give me a pat on the back saying, "Atta boy, Greg, well done." But, that's NOT what she said. What she said was, "Greg, you're giving your mom mixed signals."

I said, "What?" She said, "On one hand you're telling her it's okay to leave you, to go to Heaven, but on the other hand you're crying your eyes out, even though she didn't see you, she could hear you. She is still a mother, your mother, and she knows that if you are crying, then something is wrong, and it's not okay to go."

Hmm, "very interesting", but not funny as Arte Johnson would say.

21   *Singing and Praying*

What a blessing to have our pastor Marcus Rosa, the music leader Jonathan Statham, and the associate pastor and his wife Steven and Rebekah Wade stop by the house to sing and pray with us on occasion. Mother was in the choir at church for most of her adult life. She loved to sing the old hymns, having memorized most all the songs in the hymn book verbatim. She enjoyed the old hymns more so than the modern 'praise songs' that are sung in today's services.

Though tired and weary I feel she was glad to have the company. We gathered around her bed and began singing, mostly a'cappella. We sang the great songs of faith: AMAZING GRACE, THERE IS POWER IN THE BLOOD, ROCK OF AGES. We must have sung five or six songs in all.

Mother sang along as best as she could. For me it was a difficult thing to witness, seeing her in such a weakened state, but yet doing her utmost to join in. In God's timing, she would be singing with a new choir, a Heavenly choir, with a strong voice making her joyful noise of praise to God and God alone.

Several weeks later, Marcus, Jonathan and Steven returned for another visit, and another sing-along, this time accompanied with music playing off of YOUTUBE on someone's cell phone.

Mother was wrapped in a warm blanket while lying on the couch; her voice even more faint than before, but singing along, none the less.

These are precious memories I shall always cherish.

22   Lost Ring

Even in the seriousness of life, there are always funny moments.

Mother always wore her wedding and engagement rings. At night, she would hang them on a small nail in her bathroom. First thing every morning, she would put her rings on or have me do it for her.

As she became confined to the hospital bed, her mind ravaged by dementia, and her body seemingly all dried up, the rings became loose and were difficult to stay on her finger.

One evening as I prepared to hang her rings back on the wall, I noticed only one ring on her finger. After a casual glance inside and under the bed, I decided to wait until the next day to do a more thorough search.

So, the next day I searched and searched. I looked underneath the bed sheet, the fitted sheet, the pillow, the mattress, down on my hands and knees searching every square inch of the bedroom floor. I took the cushions off of the couch in the den, moved the couch and looked there, nothing.   I also searched the den and kitchen floors. NO RING! Next, I checked the vacuum cleaner bag. With latex gloves I went through all that was in the bag. Still no ring.

By now I was very frustrated about not finding this ring. I knew that she had both rings on the previous day, and that she had not left the bed. Where is that ring?

Except for the vacuum cleaner bag, I repeated the whole search process. Nothing. Later that evening while changing Mother's Depend, guess what appeared?   THE RING! Somehow it had slid off her finger and down inside her Depend. What a relief to finally find it. It was the last place that I would have thought to look.

23　Last Moments Together

It was late night, Thursday the 23rd of May, 2013. Even with oxygen, Mother's breathing was becoming more and more faint and shallow. I just didn't see how she could last much longer.

Like most nights, I would watch TV in the den until it was time to go to the recliner by Mother's bedside. This had been my bed for the last few months.

It was now 11 pm. Only the picture from the TV lit up the bedroom. As I settled into the recliner, my normal routine was to continue scrolling through the channels, settling on something that would help me relax before turning off the TV. But tonight I was especially tired, so after just a few minutes of channel surfing, I shut it down for the night. Almost immediately I fell asleep.

I'm not sure what woke me, well, yes, I am, but I awoke at 2 am. I got out of the recliner and turned the light on, the small light on the wall at the head of her bed. I looked at my mother and in my heart of hearts I knew she couldn't last much longer.

I put Betty LeBlanc's CD in the Bose radio/cd player, a compilation of church hymns. Betty was an accomplished piano player. Both Mother and I loved her music, and had listened many times. Mother always said, "She was better than Liberace".

I sat on the side of the bed holding Mother's hand, drawing inspiration and comfort from the music, and praying that it was peaceful for Mother, as well. There came a moment when I thought, "Do I really want to be here alone with her when she dies?" So I thought of calling Woodrow and Dollie Hobgood. Woodrow was our church deacon, and Dollie had told me to call her anytime. It would be good to have them with me in the final moments for MY comfort, MY support.

Almost as quickly as that thought entered my mind, without question, the Holy Spirit of GOD said to me, "Not just tonight, but throughout the six years with your mom, I've been right beside you. I am with you now, don't be afraid." A calm assurance came over me, and the thought of calling for support passed as we continued listening to Betty "tickle the ivories." I kissed Mom on her forehead and cheeks, telling her how much I loved her.

Her breathing was very shallow. Long breaths followed by nothing, then a short breath or two. I wondered how many more breaths she had in her. As calmly and assuredly as I could, I leaned over and whispered in her ear, "The same Jesus that will welcome you into Heaven, He is the same Jesus who will watch over me here on Earth." It's okay, Mom. Whenever you are ready. I love you."

Five minutes later, at 3 am she drew her last breath. Mother had fought life's final war with pain, and death had given way to victory.

I really can't explain my emotions at this moment. Her final war was the culmination of six long, trying, tiring, frustrating, loving, caring, and emotional years for me. The only mother I've ever known just ceased living right in front of my eyes. There were no tears.

After a brief moment of prayer, I began making phone calls. I called my sister, Larry the hospice nurse, Dollie and Woodrow, Bonnie Cothern, my cousin Martha Moak, and associate pastor Stephen Wade. They all had asked me to call, no matter the time of day or night, and so I did. They all arrived within fifteen minutes, except for Madonna who had an hour's drive, and Larry, who lived just across the Pearl River in Mississippi. It was comforting to have them there with me.

24   Visitation/Funeral

Though I remember bits and pieces of the Sunday night visitation and the Monday morning service, most of it was a blur. My pastor, Marcus Rosa, and associate pastor, Stephen Wade, did a fantastic job preparing the service, the programs, the music, and the photos of Mom and our family that would be seen on the large white screen in the church auditorium.

Special music was led by Jonathan Statham, along with Marcus Rosa and Stephen and Rebekah Wade. For me, it could not have been more perfect. Mother's life revolved around the church. She and Reggie were charter members, so it was fitting to have her visitation and the service held at our church, her church, Westside Emmanuel Baptist Church.

I know that Mother would have heartily approved of the uplifting message brought by Brother Marcus, the message of the gospel of Jesus Christ. She had raised my sister and me at the church. Eighteen years of hearing this message.

As we celebrated her HOMEGOING, it was only appropriate that all in attendance would hear, some maybe for the first time, the simple, but powerful message of how Jesus loves you, and how He wants to have a personal relationship with you.

What a comfort and strength it was for me to hear our pastor tell family and friends that this was perhaps the easiest funeral sermon he had ever preached. WHY? Because Mother, as he said, had preached her own service, simply by the way she lived her life.

So, Lennie Marie Wascom Moak, born on February 17, 1924, and dying on May 24, 2013, had indeed lived her life the best way that she knew how, by loving and giving her life away.

I witnessed Lennie's Love first hand and I loved and honored Lennie the best way that I knew how.

25   *Reflections*

When I made the decision to go back home to Bogalusa to be with my mother, it wasn't a very exciting proposition for me. She was the only reason for going back. She needed me and I guess in a way I needed her.

Bogalusa was a great place to have grown up. It was Small town USA with lots of mom and pop stores, old movie theatres, even a drive-in theatre on the outskirts of town. I had many great friends and a wonderful church.

After graduating high school, I had no intentions of sticking around. Attending different colleges and working different jobs kept me away save for occasional visits or short term stays. For some of my friends, working locally, getting married and raising a family was fine but I never had that urge to "drop anchor" in Bogalusa.

So now I find myself back and it feels like I am in a time warp. But I wasn't back in town to re- establish my childhood roots but for one reason only and that was the care of my mother Lennie.

Growing up mother and I didn't always agree on everything. What mother and son do? But she always loved me without fail.

There was a time, not to long after getting my driver's license that my friend Gary Wehmeyer and I wanted to go to a LSU football game. We had a free place to stay there in Baton Rouge and going to Tiger Stadium on a Saturday night was very exciting.

I would drive my mother's car and we would return the following afternoon. What's the problem? Well, for starters, I didn't have much driving experience and there were severe thunder storm warnings for our area. Both my mom and Mrs. Wehmeyer did not want us to go. But after endless nagging, begging and pleading we persuaded them to let us go. Although she relented, Mother didn't agree that it was the right thing to do but our persistence paid off. So with ominous clouds overhead and the wind blowing the trees back and forth, off we went. In my mind I can still see mother and Mrs. Wehmeyer standing there waving goodbye and wondering if they had made the right decision.

A stretch of the new I-12 from Covington to Hammond had not yet opened. So after traveling to Hammond via the old stretch of

Highway 190, we were about to get on the interstate for the last 50 miles or so of our journey. It was just about this time that the skies opened up and it began to rain heavily. We had not driven 5 miles when we had a flat tire. A flat, are you kidding me? I had only recently learned to drive and without a father to teach me, I had never changed a flat. Now I needed to change one in the pouring down rain. Gary had never changed a tire either. The only thing I knew to do was pull over on the shoulder of the road and start the process.

As I began to gather the jack, base and spare tire from the trunk, already soaking wet, Gary began yelling at all the cars that passed by honking their horns. The rain was not letting up and for some reason I was not able to get the jack secure into the base. It seemed like an eternity but I'm sure it was only 3-5 minutes. I became angry and frustrated and said a brief prayer, "God, please help me, help us." So it was at that moment that I noticed I had been trying to fit the jack into the hole in the base backwards and last time I checked it just wouldn't go in that way.

I turned it around and it fit perfectly, then the rest of the process was pretty straight forward and my first tire was changed fairly quickly. We continued on our trip, cold, wet and miserable for the time being but made it safely and enjoyed our football game and visit. Though the trip was against my mother's better judgement, we did make it home the next afternoon and I had learned a valuable life lesson all a result of our not agreeing.

I've always thought that over the years I was a very patient person. The nickname Granny did fit me pretty well. I usually was not in a rush and didn't rush family or friends.

In the first months and years after being home with mother, she would let me know from time to time that I needed to have a little patience. Waiting for her to get dressed, to make it out the door of the house, waiting for someone to arrive, whatever it may have been, evidently I didn't show much patience and mother let me know about it.

One of the ways that Mother thought I was being inpatient, and she enjoyed having a good laugh about it, was just after having a meal or sometimes even as we were still eating. I would ask her, "What are we going to have for our next meal?" Her thoughts of me being impatient were really me just trying to plan ahead. In the long run being with her slowed me down even more and I learned that being patient can be very helpful in many aspects of life.

Later the roles reversed and I had many laughs as Mother showed her impatience by constantly asking what's for lunch or dinner as we were still eating.

In life things usually revolve around SELF. What can be done for self and how soon. As much as I would have enjoyed playing golf 3 or 4 times a week or go to this LSU football game or that LSU baseball series or whatever it was that I wanted to do, I quickly learned that the needs of others, my mom in this situation, came before mine. Even though I may have been disappointed that I didn't get to do something or go somewhere, I knew in my heart that I had made the right decision to put her needs before mine. Today and into the future I have a peace knowing that sometimes it just not all about me.

One of the greatest surprises for Mother was her 77th birthday. She enjoyed watching Chef John Folse on TV and desired to go eat at his restaurant, Lafitte's Landing in historic Viala Plantation House in Donaldsonville. So my sister and I began planning, inviting our family and some of my close friends, Dr. Perry and Tonya Hancock, Peter Lukoff and Donna Hicks. The menu had been picked out, the cake had been chosen and more importantly we were told that If Chef Folse was at the restaurant at the time of our party he would come into the room and meet Mother and take pictures. That's just what happened. Mother was so excited. Now that was a birthday to remember!

Tis better to give than receive. A lifetime of watching my mother give of herself taught me that it is better to give of oneself than constantly hoping to get something all the time.

She gave her love freely as she and Reggie adopted my sister and I and then the love that she continued giving after Reggie's death. The times that she came to the aid of both Madonna and myself.

The love for her brothers and sisters, loving those at the church, those she came in contact with daily at her job with United Way. I loved her dearly and came to love her with a most special love in the last years with her.

For God so loved the world that He GAVE...And so as Lennie gave her all for her family and friends, sacrificially in regards to my sister and I, so I gave my all for her in the end.

The 24th of May, 2015 will be 2 years since her departure from this world. I miss her so much but again am comforted in knowing she is not suffering but is in fact whole again and in the presence of Our Lord Jesus Christ.

Lennie's Love, I am a better human being for being her son and through her guidance a son, a heir and joint heir with God and Jesus. It's ultimately through God's Love that I was able to Love Lennie

43134873R00054

Made in the USA
Lexington, KY
19 July 2015